Bournemouth

in old picture postcards

by
Catherine Rothwell

European Library – Zaltbommel/Netherlands

Acknowledgements:

Mrs. S. Black; Bournemouth Borough Council; Bournemouth Library Reference Department; Bournemouth Tourist Information Centre; Mr. J. Briggs; Stanley Butterworth; Christchurch Tricycle Museum; Collectors' Corner; Douglas Forton; William R. Hart; Lansdowne Library; Des Layton; Del Lister; Joseph W. Mason; Rosalin and Walter Mason; Pamlin Prints; Poole Maritime Museum; Railway Magazine; Railway World; Mr. E.G. Rothwell; Dr. E.J. Rothwell; Ron Severs; Jack Stasiak; Mr. R. Street; K.J. Walker; Richard West; Patricia Wilnecker; Eric Mills.

GB   ISBN 90 288 4874 6 / CIP

© 1990 European Library – Zaltbommel/Netherlands

No part of this book may be reproduced in any form, by print, photoprint, microfilm or any other means, without written permission from the publisher.

INTRODUCTION

From what now amounts to many years of research I have found the truth of the saying: 'One thing leads to another.' In collecting material for a thesis on my own town of Fleetwood-on-Wyre I was led to St. Leonard's and to Bournemouth because of the important connection with Sir Decimus Burton. It was not unusual for a seaside town in the making to have something of a struggle. Rome was not built in a day. For a short time Fleetwood and Bournemouth shared the same fate: promised growth slowed down; for some, speculation led to looming bankruptcy; but after those few short years the similarity ends. Whilst Fleetwood as a resort faded into obscurity, Bournemouth came on by leaps and bounds, never to look back, so much so that it has been written: 'There is no parallel in the history of British towns for progress such as Bournemouth.'

I have often thought that in the getting of a pier alone there is material enough in many a seaside town to make a television 'soap'; such were the jealousies, rival interests, schisms — the wheeling and dealing. There again, Fleetwood finally gained its heart's desire, but not until the 20th century, and then only to have its pier burned down, so that now the resort somewhat ignominiously has to make do with a truncated version whilst glamorous Bournemouth can support two piers and but for the cruel sea would have had three.

Great uncles and aunts painted a picture of Bournemouth to me when I was young, of stuffed birds, wax fruit, sponge fingers and hooded bath chairs on a scale unmatched by their second favourite resort, Southport, so it was a lovely surprise when I actually went. Here were real sand and sea, real cliffs, real heather, an open heathland, tall pines swaying in the sea breezes, and sunny weather that lasted all the holiday. As a nature lover I was entranced by the variety of birds, shells, flowers, ferns, mosses, and above all by the tiny, shy, green lizards popping out of rocks and basking in sunshine.

My brother's interest was in watching the trains, those great, seething, steaming monsters that charged in so furiously they made the very platforms quake. Young, middle-aged and now elderly, my husband and I have thoroughly enjoyed Bournemouth with its environs and from a store of memories recall one chef at the Durley Dene who had cooked for presidents, princesses and famous actors; an L.M.S. veteran, now 90, who had driven locomotives for 45 years and taken troops to the front line in the First World War; a sand modeller so brilliant his sculptures were to me works of art; the taste of the National Trust Christmas cake made in Bournemouth by Mary Ford; the music of the Bournemouth Symphony Orchestra; but above all, pine cones with their inseparable and incomparable scent that evokes so many more memories.

On our last visit in the glorious summer of 1989 it was the cosmopolitan quality of the town that surfaced; the International Power Boat Festival was on. After Honolulu and Nice — Bournemouth for Heat 111. Why not? In this competitive town that even has a Kite Festival, that hosts international high-speed cyclists (the first leg of the Milk Race was on 29th May), vintage and veteran vehicles covering the Daffodil Run, 16th April — well, there you have it — a pleasing accord between the old and the new, the unfailing recipe as before. In this town for all seasons one thing leads to another. It has been a pleasure to put together a picture book on such an illustrious, successful resort, and I hope both visitors and residents will enjoy the reading of it as much as I have the compilation.

Catherine Rothwell

1. Captain Lewis Dymoke Grosvenor Tregonwell who lived from 1758 till 1832 will always be known as the founder of Bournemouth. This portrait by Thomas Beach was painted in 1798 and presented to the town in 1890 by Captain Tregonwell's wife. Stationed at Poole, Tregonwell was in charge of a cavalry unit, the Dorset Rangers, patrolling between Poole and Christchurch, the area which later became Bournemouth. His task was to watch out for possible French invasion and to apprehend smugglers who at that time were an embarrassment and nuisance all around the coasts of Britain. The Captain retired from the army in 1810 and his second wife fell in love with the area. For £179 they purchased land from the Lord of the Manor for the building of a house.

2. Built in 1811, Exeter House (now part of the Royal Exeter Hotel), was first occupied by the Tregonwells in 1812. Mrs. Tregonwell decided that this was the place for herself and her family to enjoy the craze of sea-bathing. In those days it must have been an idyllic setting with a wooded chine reaching to the shore. Not far away, the only dwelling for miles, was the Tapps Arms, situated where the road crossed the Bourne river. It was the only place where travellers could obtain refreshment, the next 'public' being the New Inn at Iford. Not surprisingly, the shrewd captain knew it to be the headquarters of the smuggling that went on in the area.

PORTMAN LODGE, 1863

3. Portman Lodge, built 1811 for the accommodation of the Tregonwells' butler, was later enlarged and used as one of the Tregonwell family's own residences. Shown in this 1836 photograph, it occupied the site which later became Hampshire and Dorset bus station. Captain Tregonwell's first house was built on the west bank of the River Bourne, close to the sea. The Christchurch Enclosure Act enabled building to commence on the great Common but restricted grazing rights for the poor, which led to protest throughout the county. Fortunately, in the area which was to become Bournemouth, 425 acres were put in trust for cottagers, an area which eventually passed to the Bournemouth Corporation. On 3rd June 1922 Portman Lodge, a part of Bournemouth's history, was burned down.

MANOR ROAD.

4. Holidays in Bournemouth were really initiated by the Tregonwells who, after enjoying their splendid position exclusively for 25 years, began to advertise and attract others. The Captain had meanwhile purchased more land at £40 an acre and built a number of small cottages for letting. He advertised in the Salisbury and Wiltshire Journal, realising that a lucrative income could easily be engendered in this fashion. He let his own house to the Marchioness of Exeter (that was when house and road changed names). By 1822 he had acquired land in what is now the Cranborne Road area. Here he built a cottage for his gardener. This old postcard of Manor Road dates from the turn of the century.

On the Sands at Bournemouth   Circa 1903

5. This postcard shows the resort well recognised, with paddling, sand-castle making and bathing machines in a row in the year 1903. Bournemouth's popularity had grown from strength to strength. Following the Tregonwells, more wealthy and titled people were attracted and charmed by the resort's position. One record in the mid-1820s reads: 'I rode one day to a place called Bournemouth, a collection of hills planted by a gentleman called Tregonwell who has built five beautiful cottages which he lets... for sea-bathing. Mr. A. and I have half agreed to take one.' Tapps Arms had been rebuilt and renamed The Tregonwell Arms.

6. The loneliness of the Pine Walk at Bournemouth in this 1900s postcard of the West Cliff area gives little indication of the amount of development that had taken place in the last seventy years. Captain Tregonwell had died on 19th January 1832, aged 73, and was buried in Dorset but in 1843 his body was exhumed, brought to Bournemouth and re-interred at St. Peter's. With some ceremony he was honoured as 'the first to bring Bournemouth into notice as a watering place by erecting a mansion for his own occupation, it having been his favourite resort for many years'.

7. This six-sided Victorian pillar box, still to be seen in Bournemouth at the junction of Grove Road and Meyrick Road, is a reminder that the site of the Tregonwell Arms (pulled down in 1885) was near today's Post Office Road. The inn had become Bournemouth's first post office, George Fox, licensee, also being postmaster. This type of pillar box is now quite uncommon and was introduced in 1860, the idea of novelist Anthony Trollope who was then working as Surveyor in the Post Office. All postmasters were informed from 1840 that postage stamps would forthwith be used and were ordered to obtain an 'obliterating stamp' dipped in Red Composition. They were supplied with recipe and directions: 'Mix well 1 1b Printer's Red Ink, 1 pint linseed oil and ½ pint droppings of Sweet Oil.'

8. The great expansion programme that took place in Bournemouth's history before the mid-19th century was led by Sir George William Tapps-Gervis, son of the previously mentioned Sir George Tapps. He also could see Bournemouth's potential and his ambitious plans, although thought by some to be unrealistic, were destined for success. He chose a young Christchurch architect to design the new health resort. The Royal Bath Hotel, planned by Benjamin Ferrey (who also proposed detached villas, individual in design), was opened on the day Queen Victoria was crowned, 28th June 1838. Chine Grange Private Hotel, West Cliff, photographed in the early 1920s, is just one of hundreds that have opened in Bournemouth since then.

THE PAVILION, BOURNEMOUTH.

9. The 25 year old architect and town planner entrusted to design the new health resort had in mind trees, shrubberies, open parkland, villas, individual in design, surrounded by large gardens, but the natural advantages were to be retained as much as possible. He proposed a splendid baths to be constructed on the beach, as sea-bathing was paramount in popularity ('all kinds of bathing', included Turkish baths). Only a modest version materialised. He built the Belle Vue Hotel which later became the council's administrative centre and he much favoured a public building centrally placed for civic gatherings. His preferred site for this was where the Pavilion Theatre, opened in 1929 and shown in this 1930s postcard, was actually built.

10. The Town Hall and War Memorial feature in this postcard from July 1927 written by a happy visitor: 'We are off jaunting again, going on the beach...' Miss Smith, to whom it was written, must have wished she was there. By then the Bournemouth Municipal Orchestra's concerts were well-known. Dan Godfrey, who was knighted in 1922, continued conducting Bournemouth's orchestra until 1934. Five thousand people attended the orchestra's first performance at the Winter Gardens. As early as 1892 an Italian band had been a successful attraction on the pier. In some resorts German bands were 'all the rage', a popular song being composed about them. Symphony concerts were arranged from 1895 onwards and the Bournemouth Symphony Orchestra became known throughout Europe.

HORSESHOE COMMON AND HOLY TRINITY CHURCH, 1870

11. Bournemouth's public parks and gardens now extend for 1,500 acres. Its spacious streets and roads evoked much praise at a time when resorts were springing up all over the country. This view of Horseshoe Common and Holy Trinity Church was taken in 1870 when Christchurch was linked to Bournemouth by rail. The line from Ringwood to Christchurch was opened in 1862, then came a link between Poole and Bournemouth. 'The great connector', as railways were called, gave added impetus to both building and visitor influx. Tapps-Gervis sold land to speculators to speed construction work but he retained interests by means of long leases, he and Benjamin Ferrey determining the type of residence to be built on the land leased.

12. County Gates, Bournemouth, in 1913 is typical of what the town planner strove for in the town's appearance: wide roads, broad grass verges, trees especially pines, a feature of the town from its earliest days, with here and there large, pleasant villas, each in their own grounds. The pines and heather-clad commons had to be disturbed when building was afoot, but as much as possible these rural features were preserved, regarded by far-sighted men as essential to the dignity and well-being of town and resident. Clumps of pines encircle houses and line thoroughfares, the chief kinds being the Scots pine, the Clustered pine and the Black Austrian pine. The Corsican pine is also abundant in Meyrick and Queen's Parks and upon Horseshoe Common.

[Sweetman & Son,]   THE PINE WALK.   [Tunbridge Wells.

13. The famous Dr. A.B. Granville who had made a study of and reported on health resorts which were growing up in the 1840s, visited Bournemouth in 1841. He was impressed. At a public meeting in the town he declared: 'I look upon Bournemouth and its yet unformed colony as a perfect discovery among the sea nooks. No situation possesses so many capabilities of being made the first watering place in England.' Having received such an accolade, the town could not fail, or so it seemed. More and more visitors arrived, some very famous indeed, including Benjamin Disraeli, William Ewart Gladstone, the Prince of Wales (later Edward VII), Robert Louis Stevenson, Charles Darwin and John Keble, who actually settled. The Pine Walk, in this postcard issued by Sweetmans in the 1920s, continued as a famous promenading area from very early days, like Invalids' Walk and Fisherman's Walk.

Alum Chine, Bournemouth   Circa 1908

14. Alum Chine in 1908 has a small cluster of bathing vans ready to be drawn to the quiet beach. Thickly wooded slopes, almost to the shore, characterised the charm of the place chosen by that famous writer Robert Louis Stevenson. His house, 'Skerryvore', was situated near the top of Alum Chine but was damaged in an air raid in 1940 and later swept away although the garden remains as memorial to the author of such well-loved books as Treasure Island. Stevenson was very ill and hoped, after hearing the good reports of Bournemouth, to recover some health there. He stayed two years, but advancement of his illness, tuberculosis, eventually drove him to the South Seas where he died in Samoa.

15. The Regent Palace Hotel is an example of the huge hotels that were built in 20th century Bournemouth. Old-established hotels like Crag Hall, 'finest position in Bournemouth', Boscabel Tower, Lynton Court, Cotford Hall, Beechwood, Dalbury, Cranborne Hall and Ellerslie Mansions, in the 1920s offered accommodation at what seem today to be very low prices: winter terms 2½ guineas per week, summer 3 guineas. They offered separate tables, gas fires in bedrooms, with 'hall and landing very well heated'. The smaller establishments charged even less, averaging seven shillings and sixpence a day, full board.

Christchurch Bridge.

16. A beautiful study of the ancient Christchurch Bridge at the turn of the century, issued by Raphael Tuck, is a reminder of the link between Bournemouth and the well-known Ferrey family of Christchurch. Benjamin Ferrey, Sir George's chosen architect, had written a book on Christchurch Priory and his father was appointed Mayor in 1840. The architect went on to be in charge of restoration work at both Christchurch Priory and Wells Cathedral. Perhaps he was more proficient at church architecture. At all events, although he made a good start in Bournemouth, he was replaced by Decimus Burton in the mid-1840s, the latter having been paid off for his work in designing Fleetwood-on-Wyre in 1844. The last exponent of the British Classical School of Architecture, Burton, who had also helped his father to design St. Leonard's, brought great flair to the health resort. He too stressed the retaining of the natural advantages of Bournemouth.

Valentine & Sons, Ltd.] BOURNEMOUTH BAY, FROM BRANKSOME CHINE. [Du

17. In 1857 the prosperity of Bournemouth was in the balance. In spite of the large sums of money poured into the project and the aura of Sir Decimus blueprints, many of the latter still lay on drawing boards, for rate of growth had been disappointing, and for one heavily committed developer, Samuel Bayley, bankruptcy loomed. There were others similarly threatened. Until 1857 those who bathed in the sea had to pay Bayley for the privilege as he owned a 70 acre lease on the bathing rights over a mile of Bournemouth beach. Bayley was also one of the Town Commissioners appointed under the Town's Improvement Act passed by Parliament. This old postcard of Bournemouth Bay shows part of the stretch of beach controlled by Samuel Bayley.

OLD BOURNEMOUTH - From the Pier c 1870

COLLECTORCARD
Croydon CR0 1HW
C1190

18. Bournemouth, like other seaside towns, had to struggle hard to get its first pier; indeed, the gestation period was almost twenty years. Guide books for the town showed a pier six years before one actually materialised. The rural area of Holdenhurst and its representatives were something of a millstone as they resented money being spent, but fortunately the passing of the Bournemouth Improvement Act loosed these shackles. The Commissioners' responsibility covered an area within a mile radius of Belle Vue Hotel, from whose frontage the much dreamed of pier was to be built. This postcard from 1870 shows Bournemouth town from the very boards of its new pier, opened with much ceremony in September 1861.

19. Another view of the pier taken almost a hundred years ago, from which it is obvious that the population and the influx of visitors must have increased. The Round the Coast Guide in 1895 stated: 'The pier projects from the sea front between East and West Cliffs, at the mouth of the Bourne Valley. It is 838 feet long and 53 feet wide and was erected in 1878 at a cost of £22,000; it might also be pointed out that not a few of the residences in Bournemouth are fine mansions which elsewhere would rank as country seats.' The conflicting date concerning the pier is explained by the fact that storms swept half of it away in the early years and the full length had to be replaced.

20. The shelters at the pier head shown in this postcard from 1904 were erected in 1885 when praise was heaped upon 'the mouth of the valley which is being turned into a long strip of garden blooming with arbutus, rhododendrons and other choice shrubs under the shade of fir trees which clothe its sides'. 'Dear sister, we wish you had been here this week, we have had lovely weather', reads the message on the back of this card written in September. Medical men recommended: 'The climate of Bournemouth is most beneficial to invalids during the fall of the year and the early Spring, when it will compare favourably with many of the Mediterranean resorts.'

BOSCOMBE CHINE, 1879

21. Between two and three miles to the east of the pier, Boscombe Chine in 1875 was declared one of the favourite parts of Bournemouth. 'In the opposite direction one reaches Branksome Tower and Glen, a romantic nook fast losing its primitive wildness owing to the construction of roads and villas among the pines.' The old photograph of 1879 shows Boscombe Chine, only four years after this was printed, looking to 20th century eyes, still very rural indeed. Kinson Pottery and a site at Redlands were producing pots from clay workings from the 1850s until the 70s and 80s of this century, some of the Kinson Pottery buildings still being in existence. The earliest brickworks was at Foxholes in 1755.

22. The new Overcliff Drive, Bournemouth, is shown in a postcard from 1907, connecting Cliff Gardens with Fisherman's Walk on the boundary between Boscombe and Southbourne. Extending for 500 yards, it led from the main thoroughfare and tram route at Southbourne to the cliffs. The Cliff Gardens with tennis courts and a well-kept bowling green commanded views over the sea towards the Isle of Wight and were very popular with the visitors of those days. By the 1950s bands played in this vicinity throughout the summer. Boscombe Manor, with its associations with the Shelley family, descendants of the exiled poet, also has informal public gardens. The house became an educational establishment.

23. Wick Ferry, Christchurch, in the late 1930s was used to obtain a good view of the Priory by crossing in the ferry boat and paying one penny. Rowing boats for one or two persons were readily available for a shilling; with boatman and upto three persons the cost was five shillings. River boating on the Stour was catered for at Wick Ferry, Tuckton Creek and Iford Bridge where fleets of boats awaited visitors who usually travelled by train from Bournemouth to Christchurch. Some danger existed from thick weeds in the River Stour but boating was possible upstream to the Sheepwash at Iford Dales and in the other direction to the point where the Stour met the Avon at Christchurch.

24. This interesting notice in the grounds of Christchurch Priory can be seen to this day. Churchwardens H. Jenkins and R. Dale had it erected on 29th April 1837 as boys had made nuisances of themselves by playing in the churchyard. 'Whereas considerable damage has from time to time been done to the Windows... Tombs, Graves, Trees, Gates and in the Churchyard, notice is hereby given that persons detected in any one of the said disgraceful acts will in future be prosecuted with the utmost severity of the law.' Cattle sometimes strayed about the town and into the churchyard, whereupon the constable had the job of leading them to the town 'pound'. When claimed later by their owners, a fine was payable.

25. Corfe Castle, depicted on this postcard from the turn of the century, is shown as it looked in 1643. Every visitor to Bournemouth visited Corfe Castle, admission being only sixpence in the 1920s. Although the Saxon Chronicle records the murder of young King Edward in 978 by his own mother at Corfe, then called Corvesgate, there is no proof. Gunpowder in Cromwellian times reduced Corfe Castle to a ruin. From the keep a very fine view is obtainable over Poole Harbour, with Bournemouth beyond. The village consists of only two main streets, a tiny market place and a very interesting church which visitors were advised to see.

26. Corfe, in spite of its small size, was cited in the 19th century as a village where the traditional form of football was played in the streets 'between teams of as many who came'. This was very common in market towns all over the country and became so outrageous, noisy and damaging that Queen Victoria herself outlawed the hooligans. A law was passed by Parliament, forbidding football on the streets, and I believe it is still on the Statute Book. The coming of the railway brought visitors in their hundreds from Bournemouth to the Purbeck stone houses and castle remains and today it is estimated their numbers reach 140,000 a year.

27. Visitors also went out to Stonehenge on Salisbury Plain, travelling on from the railway stations by wagonette. This splendid card, made at the turn of the century, shows the sun or heel stone centrally and beautifully caught between the huge Sarsen blocks topped by their lintels. Erected, possibly from 1600 B.C. on, Stonehenge originally consisted of two concentric stone circles. The Altar Stone, where human sacrifice may or may not have occurred, is in line with the heel stone (known at the time of this postcard as the Friar's Heel), the first rays of the rising sun at the Midsummer Solstice striking both. Scholars still try to work out the significance, mystery and the amazing feat of erection of massive Stonehenge.

28. This view from the West Cliff, Bournemouth, was taken a hundred years ago on what was surely a public holiday, judging by the pier and beach laden with visitors. In a quarter of a century the population had increased tenfold and the boundaries extended from Hampshire into the neighbouring county. Parkstone village, for example, was in Dorset. The Guide's commentary on this photograph refers to 'Elizabethan and Gothic houses, erected at every conceivable angle and almost hidden among the foliage of trees'. Of this favourite watering place, one admirer said it was 'unique... from the ever green valley of the Bourne it stretches for miles in either direction upon sandy cliffs and the pine-clad table land of a gently curving bay'.

29. The Chines of Bournemouth are as famous as those on the Isle of Wight. Branksome Chine towards the village of Parkstone, together with Boscombe and others, by 1899, with their grouped residences were forming one continuous line from Bournemouth. The 1931 postcard shows a number of what are now vintage motor cars and much more bathing accommodation in chalets and huts by the beach, the lumbering, wheeled bathing machines having vanished. Some of the latter had to be sold in the 60s when financial problems developed, one embarrassing situation being the failure of the local bank in which the Town Commissioners had placed the municipal funds.

76 MIDDLE CHINE, BOURNEMOUTH

30. Middle Chine also in 1931 appears less developed and populous in this beautiful, sepia photograph depicting cliffs and sea. It looks ideal from a smuggler's point of view operating a hundred years earlier when one of their routes was the track along what is now Canford Road and Alder Road. Sudden increases of population concentrated on one spot can be explained by clay workings being opened. The coming of the Southern Railway to Parkstone in the late 1860s brought gangs of navvies, previously digging canals, who were called on for railway making. Parkstone, so close to Bournemouth, was then described as 'clothed with trees of the fir tribe which afford shelter from the wind and secure an equable climate'.

31. Brook, in the New Forest, must have remained unchanged in hundreds of years and even when this photograph was made in 1895, visitors were seeking it out for that reason. A well-known writer of the day said: 'The more our population grows, the more our love for nature diminishes.' He pointed out the dangers of laying waste beauty for questionable good, of sweeping away quaint streets and polluting rivers 'to make lines of dwelling houses that look like prisons'. Bournemouth's visitors took advantage of trips to the New Forest: 'Few towns can show so long or so varied a programme of excursions or possess equal facilities for visiting places of interest.' Cheap day return tickets by rail were available to Corfe, Dorchester, Isle of Wight, New Forest stations, Portsmouth, Ringwood, Swanage, Wareham, Wimborne etc.

32. Sam and Emma Briggs used the railways to reach Bournemouth in 1890, a journey made possible by saving up in a 'club'. Factories like Trickett's of Bacup set up a fund, run by the operatives, into which money was paid regularly every week. The children could join the Co-operative Wholesale Society's Penny Bank to do likewise. At any time, should emergencies arise, the money could be withdrawn. My mother one year sacrificed all of hers when a baby sister's funeral had to be paid for. Workers badly wanted their holiday when Wakes week came round, and tried hard to save enough to join a group which might travel together to the chosen resort. Blackpool could be visited any week by Northerners so people like Sam and Emma chose Bournemouth, Ilfracombe, Babbacombe, Minehead etc. This cabinet photograph of the Briggs, with Emma's ostrich-feathered hat at their feet, was taken in Todmorden.

33. Another group of northern travellers on holiday in Bournemouth. These came from Darwen in 1908 and are seated in one of the ferny chines. Some indication of the north-south divide from the days when 'travel' was relatively in its infancy is recalled by a member of this party. On the train one stranger had audibly said: 'In the north, you know, they drink out of pewter pots.' That factory workers could rise to the occasion and fit themselves out fashionably and smart is hereby shown. There were more than three million pines in Bournemouth; in 1929 10,222 being planted against 1,257 that were removed. This prevailing characteristic of the town, clumps of pines encircling houses, rows lining residential thoroughfares, was much appreciated by this group who hailed from back-to-back houses.

34. In 1924 the Town Council resolved to build the New Pavilion opposite the pier entrance on the site originally occupied by the Belle Vue Hotel. The idea was to provide for visitors and residents a round-the-year rendezvous more attractive and commodious than the Winter Gardens. Restaurants, tea rooms, balconies and a Concert Hall to seat 2,000 were included in the plans. A sprung dance floor, billiard and reading rooms were all part of the proposed amusement centre, commanding views of the Bay for miles. This artist's impression, issued on postcards which visitors sent home, gives some idea of its mingled architecture 'modern in design, with classic treatment and a suggestion of Italian in the overhanging eaves'.

35. The Pavilion and Undercliff Drive schemes were much favoured by Merton Russell Cotes who had in 1876 acquired the Bath Hotel, Bournemouth's oldest. For thirty years the energetic tycoon campaigned for improvements. His enlarged Bath Hotel was opened by the Lord Mayor of London in 1880. In 1882 plans were drawn up for the construction of Undercliff Drive. By 1890 the old Board of Commissioners had given way as Bournemouth became a borough and the Council pressed for a further Act of Parliament to include the construction of the Pavilion, although it was 35 years before the building materialised, by which time Mr. Cotes had died. This fine postcard from 1916 shows Undercliff Drive with Seabourne House on the rise (left).

36. Outside the Russell-Cotes Museum is this magnificent and interesting geological collection of 200 rocks and building stones. The specimen resting on the low cobbled wall is a large ammonite thousands of years old. Merton Russell Cotes, originally from Glasgow, presented his home, East Cliff House, and his art collection to the town. These items culled from all over the world, some priceless, form a unique treasure house, one to be proud of. The Meader collection of Victoriana is one of the most popular, but the whole display has given pleasure to generations of Bournemouth residents and visitors. Other prized collections in the town are in the Shelley Museum and the Transport Museum.

'The Windmills', Highcliffe   Circa 1900   History Overleaf

37. When Ralph Wightman wrote about Dorset in 1965 the county boundary lay west of Bournemouth, so land lying eastward was within Hampshire. In 1974 after the Local Government Boundary Commission's changes, the border shifted 10 miles east of Highcliffe, losing a triangle of the county's historically best land. This postcard from 1900 of the Windmills, Highcliffe, with 'Highcliffe Motor Garage' on the right, shows the General Store and Post Office. The Frampton family were interested in windmills, Highcliffe being called Newtown in 1888. On the site of the garage a Methodist church was built, the land being given by Mr. Frampton.

38. On Horse Shoe Common a solitary, long-gowned lady in 1901 walks in what are still rural surroundings. Many hundreds of years before, Christchurch and Poole were already boroughs of note, long-established, but Bournemouth had yet to rise in the tracts of Common that lay between. Wild-fowlers, or smugglers evading the customs officers were the only wanderers on this wild heath. In the reminiscences of the Earl of Malmesbury he tells that in 1826 he 'shot a black cock on the very spot where St. Peter's Church now stands'. St. Peter's can be seen in the distance on this lovely postcard issued by J. Welch and Sons.

39. St. Peter's Church and the entrance to Bournemouth Arcade are the subjects of this holiday postcard from 1907. In 1845 the Reverend Alexander Morden Bennett became the first vicar of St. Peter's. He commissioned G.F. Street to build the church which was completed in 1879. Many famous people are buried in the churchyard where also in a casket is the heart of the poet Percy Bysshe Shelley. The Bournemouth Arcade, when this card was issued, was a glass-covered way 20 feet in width and 200 feet long, leading from the old Christchurch Road to Gervis Place and the Pleasure Gardens.

St. Peter's Church and entrance to Bournemouth Arcade
Circa 1907

40. Poole Quay on a 1910 postcard shows the Scandinavian three-masted barque Albege, a timber ship, in the centre. The timber was off-loaded through the opening under the bow of the ship, using horse-drawn wagons, one of which can be seen, dwarfed by the size of the vessel alongside. Poole was a landing for the Norsemen in the 10th century and into its harbour sailed Canute with his fleet, making for Wareham on the western end. C.R. Penney and Company sold ropes and canvas in their sack store situated next to the Poole Arms which dispensed 'Marston's celebrated extra stout and genuine wines'. Chandlers' premises and sail lofts lined the quay.

41. Off Handfast Point are some pinnacles called the Old Harry Rocks, one being much smaller than the other. In these chalk cliffs near Bournemouth are caves once used by smugglers, the best known being Parson's Barn. This stretch of coast could be viewed by steamboat when this postcard was written from Boscombe in the 1920s. Traces of early civilisation have come to ligth on the cliff tops. Pottery sherds have turned up in gardens, palaeolithic axes and neolithic remains at Haymoor and Rossmore Roads. The remains of Roman encampments are to be found in the New Forest. At Longham the skull of Bournemouth Woman was unearthed in 1932 and the remains of a prehistoric forest, in the making of the 1868 jetty attached to the pier.

BOSCOMBE LOOKING EAST.

COPYRIGHT LP 450

42. The postcard showing Boscombe looking east was taken about twenty years later when it had become one of the eleven municipal wards of Bournemouth. In the early days it was neglected, consisting of a few cottages inhabited by labourers from a nearby brickfield. The site of a humble public house was replaced by villas, hotels and tree-shaded gardens, by the 1900s, Chine Gardens replacing the brickfields. Christchurch Road is the main thoroughfare between Boscombe and Bournemouth, another connecting road being East Cliff Drive. The Chine was once spanned by a rustic bridge, which was replaced by the concrete structure shown in another postcard.

43. This beautiful photograph published by J.E. Beale of Bournemouth is one in a series of postcards dating from about 1910 which reveal the full extent of Bournemouth's mile and a half long pleasure gardens. The town's green spaces are derived mainly from natural surroundings. To create their 'Forest City by the Southern Sea', the councillors and commissioners before them used patches of ancient forest and in the open spaces improved on Nature by clever planting of flowers and shrubs. In the mild climate camellias, azaleas, bamboo and Mexican orange flourish. Some villas can grow fig trees in their sheltered gardens.

VIEW FROM TERRACE MOUNT, 1881

44. The 1881 view from Terrace Mount shows how the town had grown from the days of the Tapps Arms. In the 15th century this area was indicated on the map as simply the mouth of the River Bourne, within the west bay at Christchurch, 'one quarter of a mile in length and void of habitation'. The wealthy Henrietta, wife of Lewis Tregonwell living at Mudeford, changed all that when she expressed a desire to have a house built on land where later grew up the town of Bournemouth. Its economic growth aided by the railways showed a population increase from 6,507 in 1871 to 60,000 in 1900. Today Bournemouth has over 152,000 residents.

45. The sweet-scented pines were said to be a cure for tuberculosis, which was why Robert Louis Stevenson had a house in Alum Chine. Here he wrote 'Prince Otto' and 'Kidnapped', but by 1888 had moved off to the South Seas. Sanatoriums were built and bathchairs introduced; indeed the town was dotted with bath chair parks, the pullers waiting in thatched shelters to be hired. One postcard shows a bath chair drawn by a donkey and I am told this was usual. The postcard from 1917 shows the Pergola at the Herbert Home, with three nurses seated at the end. G.E. Bridge and Company advertised in the 1915 Directory of Bournemouth: 'Invalid transport service — Motor Ambulance, full-length stretcher fitted but has the appearance of a private limousine.'

The Pergola, Herbert Home. Bournemouth.

46. 'The city of Pines' celebrated its centenary in 1910, the date of this postcard showing the Undercliff Drive and Huts, Bournemouth. Queen's park, Talbot Woods, Meyrick Park and the Golf Links constructed in 1924 further enhanced areas, but the original state of wild gorse and heather was often left untouched. Talbot Woods, a tract of pine forest lying north of the Upper Pleasure Gardens, could be approached across the Golf Links. The railway running in a deep cutting did not detract from this mile-long length of pines, but subsequent building in the 20th century has done so.

Children's Canal, Pleasure Gardens, Bournemouth.   *Published by A. Sear, West Bournemouth.*

47. In 1905 this postcard was sent to a friend in Somerset. It is published by A. Sear of West Bournemouth and shows the Children's Canal in the Pleasure Gardens. Winston Churchill sailed his toy yacht here as a little boy and made a daring leap in one of the chines that could have changed the course of history if it had failed. A Noddy train along the Undercliff delights modern children. Ninety years ago Empress Eugenie was impressed by Bournemouth's candle illuminations on the water when 20,000 coloured glass jars were fitted with a single candle in each. I understand that jars are still wheeled to the Lower Gardens four times a year, to be hung on large wooden frames.

48. A postcard written to Bacup in the early 1930s shows the Square and Gardens, traffic centre of the town. Many roads converged onto the Square, the most interesting perhaps being Old Christchurch Road, a shop-lined thoroughfare down which the trams ran to Lansdowne, a winding road that gave way to straight Christchurch Road and Boscombe. At Lansdowne was built the Municipal College and Central Library in 1912 at a cost of £45,000 in a commanding position on Meyrick Road. Its clock tower can be seen and heard all over town. Only a year later the Theatre Royal was advertised as 'possessing the most luxuriously fitted foyer in the country'.

49. The electric lift at East Cliff opposite Meyrick Road is so high a tremendous curve of the Bay can be seen, but a sufferer from vertigo would find the sight trying. This postcard from early 1920 gives a good impression of an almost sheer drop. The making of the lift revealed some interesting geology. Lignite, the metamorphosed wood of ancient trees, was revealed; pure pipe-clay occurs and in these purer clays the best specimens of fossil leaves are found. A thick bed of plateau gravel was found to cap the cliffs but the base consists of a bed of dark clay containing large amounts of iron pyrites. There was another lift provided at West Cliff beyond the bathing cabins.

F. Frith & Co., Ltd.]   HENGISTBURY HEAD.   [Reigate.

50. Hengistbury Head, dividing the bays of Bournemouth and Christchurch, was part of the area lost in Local Government Boundary reorganisation. In prehistoric times there was a large, fortified earthworks and ancient remains came to light by excavation: pit dwelling of Neolithic times; flint weapons; Bronze Age pottery and urns. Gold, amber and a collection of 4,000 gold, silver and bronze coins have also been found here. It has a fine beach below and in the days of smuggling Hengistbury Head was notorious. 30-40 wagons with 200 horsemen alongside were reported as coming over the mighty Head in broad daylight. Severe penalties did not deter the law breakers, with whom the general public sided.

51. Another beautiful 1910 postcard, 'View from the Pier', in the year Lorna Doone was produced at the Pavilion. Admission in 1929 was only twopence to this popular pier, a book of 12 tickets one shilling and eightpence. A whole season ticket to Bournemouth and Boscombe piers could be had for 15 shillings and when the Municipal Band was playing a seat in the enclosure cost threepence. In 1909 landing stages for the steamers were improved for this important sea traffic so popular with visitors, although people liable to sea sickness considered the promenade along the pier tantamount to going to sea without the disadvantages.

S.S. "Brodick Castle" off Bournemouth Pier   Circa 1905

52. The Brodick Castle is shown off the pier in 1905 when paddle steamers were plying all around our coasts. Navigated by sextant and the captain's considerable experience, they operated from the health resorts in the 1860s, continuing for 100 years. In 1886 the 'Bournemouth' of Bournemouth, Swanage and Poole Steam Packet Company set out alongside the 'Weymouth', both bound for Torquay. On the return journey fog came down and the unfortunate 'Bournemouth' went on the rocks at Portland Bill, a foggy time, for two days later, the 'Queen' also ran on rocks.

53. Another fine postcard of S.S. Brodick Castle in 1905 signed Eric ('Can you see us, this is the boat we went to Southsea on'). The 'Empress' in 1881 was the first steamer to make the trip to Torquay and back in one day, taking 13 hours. The Bournemouth company who owned 'Lord Elgin', 160 feet long, 'Brodick Castle' and 'Windsor Castle', both over 200 feet long, shared local steamer traffic with the Cosens Company from Weymouth. The iron pier of 1880 had as many as four paddlers along at a time during busy summer seasons. Boscombe and Southbourne piers, when they opened, gave more facilities, although Southbourne's contribution was short-lived after 'Lord Elgin' had inaugurated a run.

54. Here we have 'Monarch', the best known steamer on local routes, on a beautiful summer's day, to be precise, 27th August 1930. For 62 years she plied around Bournemouth waters, ending her career in 1950. Distinguished by thin, black-topped, yellow funnels and small paddle boxes, in her early days she ran cross-Channel trips to Cherbourg and up to the First World War made trips also to Alderney in the Channel Islands. Seated in serried rows, it must have been a good way to acquire a sun tan, but even in 1930 black umbrellas are still warding off the sun's rays.

55. Sea-going craft were sometimes visible from Bournemouth, sailing to and from Southampton. This very old photograph shows S.S. Servia, 7,392 tons, built at Clydebank in 1881 and owned by Cunard Line. With her raked masts and elegant lines she was a beautiful vessel. In later years the Queen Mary and Queen Elizabeth were in waters off Bournemouth, making for the Ocean Terminal which opened in July 1950. The first R.M.S. Queen Elizabeth, 1,031 feet long, 118 feet broad, weighed 83,673 tons. This Cunard White Star Liner was once the pride of the fleet. The Q.E.2 came into service in 1969.

56. Six miles of beaches, some of the safest and cleanest in Great Britain (only 17 resorts have been awarded the blue flag to fly at the Pier Head, and Bournemouth is among them) are to be enjoyed. This 1912 postcard of the West Cliff Sands and Bungalows shows part of them, with cliffs in the distance. Buckets and spades are in evidence with other seaside paraphernalia: deck chairs, parasols, shady hats and towels. The enterprising John Elmes set up a business in Bournemouth which grew into an internationally-known department store. In 1885, the early days, he stocked 'buckets, spades, parasols, walking sticks and children's boats'. Beale's was the first store to have a resident Father Christmas.

57. Edward VII built what has been called 'a love nest' for his actress friend Lillie Langtry, 'the Jersey lily', at Bournemouth. The house is now a hotel, Langtry Manor, which ranks the Edward VII suite with its huge bed and fireplace rather highly. On the minstrels' gallery are carved the words 'They say, what say they? Let them say'. The soulful-eyed Lillie herself, photographed in her role as Cleopatra, for which she personally hired the theatre, might well be uttering those words. Aubrey Beardsley and John Galsworthy stayed in Bournemouth and the town remembers thankfully photographer Robert Day who recorded so much of its history.

58. To many, Christchurch Priory was the landmark first seen when approaching Bournemouth, 'the land of long and glorious summer holidays'. The 11th century Priory has a beautiful story attached to its building. A site was chosen but mysteriously and miraculously each night building materials were moved to another site until eventually, believing it to be divine guidance, the second site was decided upon. Each day a stranger helped the men but he neither spoke to nor ate with them, nor did he receive any pay. After a particularly difficult beam was put into place the stranger, believed to be the Carpenter of Nazareth, was never seen again. So the old name of Twynham was changed to Christchurch. This frail photograph from the 1880s is one of the two oldest in the book.

59. Adjoining the Priory this second oldest photograph taken by A. Malle of Church Street and later issued as a postcard shows the ruins of Norman House. It reveals one of the few examples of Norman domestic architecture in existence; a huge fireplace connects with the circular chimney. The remains of the east and west walls of the Norman Keep, 20 feet high and 10 feet thick, were also originally built by the Earl of Devon in the 12th century, but he actually lived in the Norman House. Mudeford Quay at Christchurch is the centre of the local sea-fishing industry, expressed by a golden weather vane in the shape of a fish on top of the Priory Tower. Samuel Taylor Coleridge praised the bracing air of Christchurch Harbour which is almost landlocked.

60. Locomotive Alfred the Great, 70009, heads the Bournemouth Belle Pullman past Battledown flyover on the down journey, although the use of Britannia Class locomotives did not last long in the 1950s on the western lines of Southern Region. What an exciting journey it was! The inaugural Bournemouth Belle left Waterloo on 5th July 1931, pulling one of the first all-steel cars introduced in 1929. In November 1967 Southern Region commissioned the major part of its Bournemouth line re-signalling scheme. Although the architecture of the Railway Station is not the type to excite a purist, the Preservationists seek to keep it intact.

61. This postcard shows Bournemouth Junior Railway Club in 1946 visiting Bournemouth Locomotive Depot. The group includes, top row, second from left: the President, the Rev. A. Cunningham Burley; bottom, standing, fourth from right, Alan Trickett, who was to become Chairman. The Club reached its 30th year in 1973. By 1964, on its 21st anniversary, it was simply the Railway Club as most members had grown up by 1953. The amazing growth of Bournemouth around the turn of the century was due mainly to the presence of the railway. A fast service to London's Waterloo station, three times an hour, taking 97 minutes, is what today's traveller enjoys and there are regular services to Scotland and other parts.

62. W. Smith and Sons, butcher's shop, Old Christchurch Road, at Christmas time about 1904. With knives at the ready, the two sons in their classic aprons look very business-like. An array of poultry, meat, rabbits, game, sausages and brawn would no doubt all be gone by Christmas Eve. The great hooks above the window for display and the large gas lamp were part of the fittings of that day. In some butchers' shops whole pigs were scrubbed and laid out on the slab, orange in mouth. The interior had clean sawdust regularly scattered on the marble floor.

63. It is July 1923 and another happy group is being recorded at Mrs. Stone's, 'Rochdale', Tregonwell Road, Bournemouth. The travelling photographer had a good trade going between hotels and on board the 'Monarch', supplying photographic souvenirs for visitors. Planning the day before them, some may be off to the Isle of Wight, Christchurch, Lyndhurst, Poole, Winchester, Wimborne, or considering 'Any more for the Skylark?' A twelveseater open launch called Skylark, run by 'Ginger' Bolson from Alum Chine, was forerunner of the Bolson family empire. By the date of this photograph Ginger had opened a boatyard at Poole and greatly enlarged his fleet of pleasure boats.

64. Branksea Island, as it was called in 1895, at the mouth of Poole Harbour, is six miles in circumference and well wooded, an island that once belonged to Cerne Abbey and was the abode of a hermit. Branksea Castle is shown in the photograph of that date, erected as defence in Henry VIII's reign. Colonel Waugh occupied and furnished the castle in 1890 and opened pits to work the excellent potter's clay there deposited. He built a pier, laid a tramway and put up St. Mary's Church, but his venture failed. This old photograph gives a general view of the castle.

65. An old postcard from the 1890s of the beautiful resort of Lucerne is most appropriate to old Bournemouth as, after many years of association they have become twinned towns. Bournemouth prided itself on seeking a town whose accent also was on beautiful surroundings. Frequently visitors from the English resort, after staying in Lucerne, came away with the words of the Chief Executive of Bournemouth Council on their lips: 'You arrive as a stranger and leave as a friend.' This beautiful study which I purchased on my visit is by Casp Hirsbrunner, showing famous Lake Geneva and a paddle steamer not unlike 'Monarch'.

66. The western exit from Bournemouth by rail is shown in the 1950s with a group of the famous pines in the foreground. This photograph by K.G. Walker has captured a steam engine on the right. Train spotting was at its height and some small boys preferred to spend their holiday on the railway platforms rather than on the beach, to the despair of parents, including my own. The Pines Express, in the 1930s as famous as The Devonian, was originally a joint London and North Western and Midland service, beginning its journey at Liverpool. The last 80 miles of the journey over Southern metals brought the Pines Express into Bournemouth West at 4.35 p.m., a seven-hour journey from Liverpool, 254 miles away.

67. Whereas in the early days Brighton visitors were criticised as 'more shameless than at any other place', Bournemouth, the fashionable health resort, seemed able to maintain its social aloofness. As a health resort, the town, with its heavy concentration of old people and private nursing homes, felt it had 'visitors of a better sort'. The exclusiveness of King's Drive in July 1908 does seem to bear this out. The coming of the 1914-1918 Great War led to 1,300 aliens being expelled and residents criticised the playing of German music. Over 15,000 troops were billeted in Bournemouth in 1915 and no lights were to be visible from the sea.

68. Haywood Mill, Boldre, in the New Forest, which visitors to Bournemouth included in their trips. This picturesque postcard issued by Mrs. C.A. Kitcher, Stationer, from the Post Office, 47 Commercial Road, Bournemouth, was written by Lizzie in April 1905. The party went on to Bramshaw Wood, containing the famous twin beeches and its churchyard with ancient yews, which used to be in two counties before boundaries were changed. The church displays a memorial to seven local men who died in the Titanic disaster.

69. The Rufus Stone at Canterton Glen in the New Forest was erected in 1745 by Earl de la Warr, but defacement by the public caused it to be encased in iron by 1841. This photograph was taken in 1897. It is a moot point whether the much disliked William II, nicknamed 'Rufus', was accidentally killed by Walter Tyrrell on 2nd August 1100. Accounts say that the hunting party of five continued their sport until late afternoon when the King wounded a stag. Almost immediately another stag broke cover, at which Tyrrell (earlier presented with two arrows by the King: 'To the best marksman, the best arrows') shot. Glancing from a tree, the arrow struck the King dead. Tyrrell fled to France by way of Tyrrell's Ford.

70. Many old freehold cottages in the New Forest still have turbary, pannage and grazing rights attached to them. Pannage is the right to turn pigs out for six weeks when the acorns and beech mast have fallen in autumn. Such rights belong to the chimney and hearthstone, not to the individual. This postcard from 1906 shows Miss Braddon's New Forest home at Bank. She was a successful late-Victorian novelist, real name Mrs. Maxwell, who died in 1915. Perhaps her most popular and sensational novel was Lady Audley's Secret.

NEW FOREST PONIES V3154

71. The ponies of the New Forest are as great an attraction today as when this postcard was printed in 1930. 'The ponies in the New Forest are perfectly sweet and look so healthy and well groomed', reads the message from Edith. Great numbers, wiry, sure-footed and healthy, thought to be descended from the jennets which swam ashore from the wrecks of the Spanish Armada, are carefully monitored by New Forest rangers who must keep the stock pure bred, culling if necessary and preserving trees and herbage needed for their well being.

72. Many postcards exist of the character Brusher Mills, the snake catcher in the New Forest, but this one dating from 1906 is particularly interesting as it shows what is either his habitation or a charcoal burner's hut. He was equipped with bag, stick and can, but would not be a popular character today as snakes in Britain are becoming endangered species. In those days they were fed to the large, dangerous snakes in London Zoo. The 'capital' of the New Forest is Lyndhurst from where seven roads radiate: Bournemouth, Southampton etc. Here is the Verderers' Hall where meetings are held six times a year, a court surviving from the days of the Norman conquest. A great parish was once Eling where Cobb, the King's Fletcher, held territory known as Coblands. His service was to supply arrows when the Kings came hunting.

73. East Cliff at Bournemouth, 19th August 1904, looks very busy, with lots of rowing boats available to take people into the bay. There are wheeled bathing machines still in evidence (some persisted until the 1920s). From Belle Vue Terrace this correspondent writes: 'We are having a delightful holiday and are both better.' It is interesting to recall that novelist Thomas Hardy called Bournemouth 'Sandbourne' in his novels 'The Hand of Ethelberta' and 'Tess of the D'Urbervilles'. Horace Annesley Vachell's 'Blinkers' also is set in Bournemouth.

74. The circus comes to town in this 1894 photograph, travelling circuses and fairs arousing great excitement in the days when there was much less entertainment available. One famous circus, Wombwell's, brought 17 elephants and W.J. Day's photograph is still in Bournemouth Library to prove it. This photograph shows all the excited children following in the rear. Patricia Wilnecker states that circuses and fairs were the earliest forms of public entertainment, Parkstone being well catered for. Lord Sanger's, Bertram Mills' and Billy Smart's circuses drew large crowds. The fairgrounds had sideshows and roundabouts, with gingerbread the favourite sweetmeat.

VIEW FROM ST. PAUL'S TOWER, 1888

75. This 1888 view is from the tower of St. Paul's in the days when streets were almost devoid of traffic. Local names which have vanished since the town's population explosion were then current. Sugar Knob was a hill north of Gwynne Road; Bribery Island was near the Gas Works, a group of smallholdings owned by Lady Wimborne. She was said to sell or let them only to people who voted for one of her sons in the elections. Wallywack was the nickname for Wallisdown, whilst Heavenly Bottom referred to a marshy area in Churchill/Albert Roads where lived gypsies, some of whom peddled their wares outside Beale's Fancy Fair in 1883, as the store was then named.

76. Christchurch, Wick Ferry, in the late 1890s presents an idyllic scene. Bathing and fishing are popular and the cycling craze which arrived in the 1880s is apparent by the number of bicycles leaned against the wattle fence. All, however, was not harmony in Bournemouth, for in the 1880s when the town hoped to gain Borough status some people objected. On 5th November 1884 over 500 people gathered, lighted tar barrels were rolled up and down, the police superintendent 'pelted with mud, stones and thick sticks' and £200 worth of windows smashed in 14 shops and three public houses.

77. At the time of this delightful street scene in Wareham's West Street, everyone (all 15) wanted to be on the photograph. Grocers, tanners, and potter's assistants were paid but a few shillings weekly. A cloakroom attendant in Bournemouth and similar council employees drew a wage of ten shillings. Indeed, the Borough Surveyor received only £500 a year. Gardeners, beach inspectors and lamplighters were paid one guinea, as were the 28 Bournemouth carters employed in 'house scavenging'.

THE BAY FROM DURLEY CHINE, BOURNEMOUTH. C.M.238.

78. The Bay from Durley Chine was portrayed on cards like this in the 1940s issued in the 'Sun Ray Series'. 'The sun has been very hot indeed, but we keep cool by going in the sea,' wrote Alice to her friend in Bolton. The cliffs and foreshore at Durley Chine were always popular with holidaymakers, many still coming from the north and north-west of England as these postcards show. The land with the chine was the property of William Dean in 1805 and the name, which is thought to derive from Durley near Bishop's Waltham, appeared on a local map about that time.

Entrance to the Pier, Bournemouth   Circa 1909

79. The clock at the entrance to the pier, here shown in 1909, was presented by Horace Davey who became Lord Davey, member of Parliament for Christchurch. He also represented Bournemouth. Landaus and bicycles are much in evidence on what is obviously a lovely summer's day. Bournemouth was looking to the following year, 1910, and aiming to commemorate its first hundred years in grand style as no other British town could equal Bournemouth's progress in that time. An attempt was made in 1910 to capture the carnival spirit of Nice and the Riviera in confetti battles (Meyrick Park) and giant floats which came over specially from the Continent.

80. Branksome Dean Chine was my brother's favourite in the years of this postcard before the Second World War. Lovely wooded areas, bathing huts and easy access into a less polluted sea made for a carefree, beneficial stay. Note the vintage motor vehicle delivering supplies for the tearoom, so handy for the shore. Even more leafy, Alum Chine had a history of 16th century mining. The Lord of the Manor of Canford discovered alum on his estate and set up production as large quantities were used in the tanneries. Unfortunately it was not a success; the Baron was ruined and died in poverty. The investors lost their money.

81. One visitor, a Preston burgher who helped to organise the 1901 Preston Guild, used to stay at Newlyn's Royal and Imperial Hotel, renowned for its excellent organisation and attention to visitors. Mrs. Leonie Newton assisted her husband, Henry, in the management of the hotel and as mayoress, played an active role in the furtherance of the resort. The Preston Guild link brought an exchange of visitors. Henry was an alderman and the couple were typical of the age: successful, prosperous, but not indifferent to people in the community less fortunate than themselves.

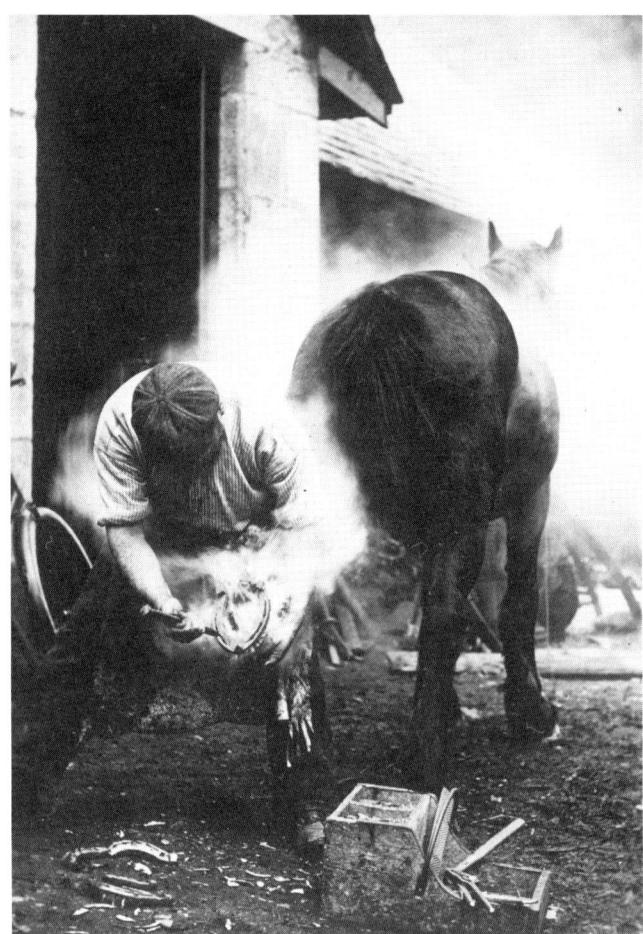

82. Mr. Bligdon, the Parkstone blacksmith, was a busy man in the days when horses were universally needed: on the roads to haul carts; in the fields for ploughing, harrowing and drawing loads; and for horseback riders. Those were the days of the heavy horses, great Shires, which are now the subject of special museums of which Dorset's is one. This postcard series, though not including Mr. Bligdon, was sent all over England in the 1920s, when people began to realise that with the advent of the petrol engine, rural crafts were on the way out.

83. The largest library of chained books is at Hereford Cathedral with 2,000 volumes but this one at Wimborne Minster near Bournemouth has been of great interest for many years to visitors from the famous resort. Cartmel Priory, Lancashire, also has a library of chained books. The postcard dates from October 1904. Sometimes individual chained books on stands are found, indicating the value and esteem in which these beautifully illuminated and embellished manuscripts are held. Books were chained before the Reformation and afterwards it appears to have been even more necessary.

The Old Clock Wimborne Minster.

84. Beneath the 15th century tower of Wimborne Minster is a Purbeck marble Norman font, but one of the most interesting items is the Orrery or Astronomical Clock constructed about 1325 by Peter Lightfoot, the monk who made a similar clock at Wells Cathedral. He came from Glastonbury Abbey. The sun, moon and stars are depicted as revolving round the earth, the sun completing circuit in 24 hours, when its position marks the hour. Each day the clock, worked by weights and pendulum, has to be wound. It is indeed a wonderful piece of mechanism and modern, since we have reverted to 24-hour timings!

85. An unusual photograph taken about 1898 by flashlight, showing the interior of a Victorian Boarding Establishment at Boscombe. The curved gas light bracket, aspidistra, furnishing, heavy wallpaper pattern, and the clothing of the lady and two girls, the Misses Howarth (lace jabot, velvet, long silk gown) make this a true period piece. Boscombe at this time was probably less expensive than Bournemouth. With a climate described as temperate all the year round and free from fog, people were prepared to travel some distance to Bournemouth and Boscombe. The Purbeck range of hills protected the town from the worst of wind and weather, yet South West breezes could be enjoyed.

86. By the 1950s the appearance of the Square, hub of the town, had become more crowded with buildings. Trolley buses were running and the variety of shops had increased. From here present-day guided tours are conducted by Wally Driffield. Two thousand acres of gardens 'threaded end to end by the Bourne Stream' beginning at Coy Pond, through Upper and Central Gardens, where bands played, were thronged all year round. Today Bournemouth spends one million pounds per annum to control litter and there is a great watering of flowers every morning. In 1987 the town was Number One Floral City.

87. Near Wimborne are the Knowlton Circles, a historically ancient henge monument. The postcard, which dates from the early years of this century, shows the Saxon church of St. Martin's at Wareham. Board Residence at The Yews was supplied by Mrs. Crocker who had her own postcards printed, showing the elegant exterior of a large Georgian house and the garden at the rear, large enough to include a tennis court. There were benches for visitors to rest under shady trees and a smartly dressed gardener with an antiquated mowing machine keeping the lawns trimmed. The Yews seems to have been a good place to stay.

88. This was a well-known Hotel Sign which visitors saw in the New Forest, the Trusty Servant at Minstead, just under a mile from the Rufus Stone. It is a curious sign, a copy of that in Winchester College which refers to the parts of the composite creature. The inscription below explains, too long to quote in full, but examples are: The Porker's snout 'not nice in diet shews', the Padlock Shut, 'no secrets He'll disclose'. Swiftness in errand, 'the stags' feet declare'. Labouring tools and sword to protect his master from harm are all part of 'this emblematic figure', a perfect but eerie servant.

LILY ELSIE

89. Lily Elsie, on a card postmarked July 1908, appeared on the London stage but was later part of Bournemouth's entertainment. Leading actors, singers and actresses appeared at Bournemouth's Second Town Hall when it opened as a theatre. The Pavilion had a coloured postcard produced by A. Vivian Mansell and Company Ltd., Fine Art Dealers, after its opening in 1929. Bournemouth, 'where the season never ends', draws crowds to its Symphony Orchestra and the Bournemouth Sinfonietta. The Theatre Royal in Albert Road, built 1882, could seat 1,000 people and Boscombe had its Grand Pavilion Theatre in Christchurch Road. On our most recent visit, dancer Wayne Sleep was appearing at the Pavilion Theatre with a dynamic supporting company.

90. All these lovely dresses at what may have been a Parkstone wedding (the postcard turned up locally and a splendid copy of it was made) are crowded into a backyard; not to mention the wonderful hat creations! Dating probably from the days of Queen Alexandra, it is not surprising to read in old directories that as many as a score of dressmakers worked in comparatively small towns. The photographer, who has entirely draped the back wall to hide brickwork, would have a heavy plate camera on a wooden tripod, with a large black cloth thrown over to keep out light.

The Pier Approach and East Cliff, Bournemouth. 1875.

91. Kelly's Directory of Bournemouth, Christchurch and Poole, with Longfleet, Parkstone etc. for 1913-14, printed about the time of this enchanting postcard showing the Pier Approach and East Cliff, is full of information. We learn the following: Bright's Stores had over forty departments, operating at Old Christchurch Road, Gervis Place and the Arcade; The Bournemouth Graphic, an illustrated weekly, cost one penny every Friday; Curtis and Sons, Removal contractors, used Burrell steam engines to tow two vans for long-distance removals; and the Reliance Family Laundry's high-class work was 'noted for flannels' – all of which builds up a picture of those days.

92. A favourite comic song sung by Fred Coyne, dedicated to the Prince of Wales, later Edward VII, was called 'The Velocipede'. Christchurch Tricycle Museum specialises in all such types: the Trivector from 1819; the Velocimanipede; the Quadront; the Boneshaker tricycle and the Velocipedienne, the last mentioned, a costume for ladies to hide 'working knees and effectively cover feet and ankles'. The Cooliecycle of 1882 was sold to Indian princes. 'While going through Bournemouth and on to Christchurch, I was struck by the unusual number of tricycles I passed, most of them hired to visitors, ridden by men and maidens, young men and children.' The oil painting, transferred to postcard, gives a good idea of the tricycle of more than a century ago. Obviously a race is on. ('On the new velocopede so gaily, you'll see the people riding daily.')

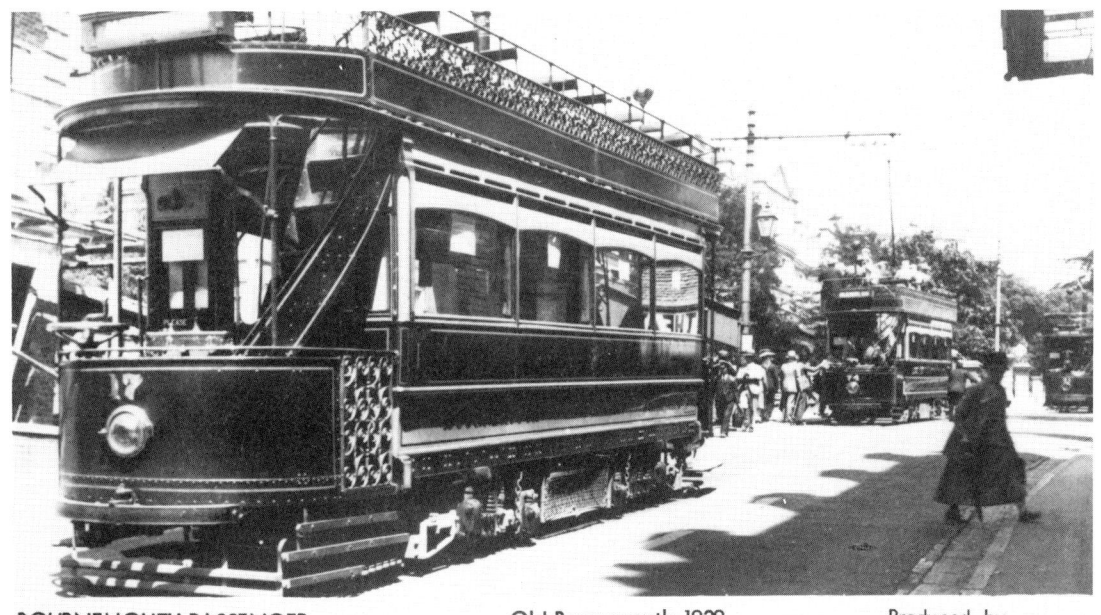

BOURNEMOUTH PASSENGER TRANSPORT ASSOCIATION
Postcard Series No. 17

Old Bournemouth 1929
Richmond Hill
(By Courtesy of Bournemouth Transport)

Produced by
Pamlin Prints
Croydon

93. A 1929 tram, number 17, is shown in this postcard, but as early as 1840 horse-drawn coaches called in at Bournemouth each day at noon. These 'Emerald' coaches went on to Southampton, Poole, Dorchester and Weymouth. Even earlier, in the 1830s, some hotels made their own arrangements to meet visitors at the nearest railway stations in the New Forest (Holmsley and Hamworthy). Bournemouth man Henry Laidlaw was prepared to go long distances at any time. A wagonette service at the turn of the century from Boscombe was popular with visitors.

BOURNEMOUTH PASSENGER TRANSPORT ASSOCIATION
Postcard Series No. 401

WILTS & DORSET BRISTOL 'K'
at Bournemouth 1953
(Photo: G.O. Pearce - B.P.T.A. Collection)

Produced by
Pamlin Prints
Croydon

M2408

94. The Wiltshire and Dorset K. omnibus is shown at Bournemouth in 1953. Today's Yellow Buses and Coaches fleet has fine double and single-decker buses providing services, but many people lamented the passing of the silent, clean trolley buses shown in some of the postcards. As traffic grew more congested and electricity more expensive it was apparent that, like the trains, they must go. The last trolley bus journey was made from Bournemouth Pier in the late 1960s. Some old trolley buses are preserved for the visitor to see at the Transport Museum.

95. An inventor, William Jeans, who had a small factory in Bridge Street, Christchurch, in the 1880s, offered a reward of £500 to anyone locating an originial tricycle like the one illustrated, which had been manufactured by the Zephyr Cycle Company of Coventry. The Coventry Lever Tricycle was ridden to Coventry from Christchurch in 1977, rasing £700 for charity. Another Christchurch inventor was Sir Donald Bailey at the Experimental Bridging Establishment there in 1940. During the Second World War over 260 miles of the bridge were manufactured and played a part in eventual victory.

96. This moss-grown sundial in the churchyard of the Priory at Christchurch is engraved in memory of H. Gregory Neary of India House, London. Alongside are other distinguished names: Field Marshal Hugh Henry Rose; Lord Strathnairn, born 1801, died 1885, contemporary of the Reverend Zachary Nash, curate of Christchurch Priory. Margaret, Countess of Salisbury, erected a chantry here as her own resting place but the story of her entire family was one of tragedy. She was the butt of Henry VIII's vicious rage and was buried in the 'cemetery for traitors' in the shadow of the Tower of London: 'Margaret of Salisbury, the last of the proud race of Plantaganets'.

97. Showing the nearby sign of H. Brooks, picture restorer and picture framer, the Close Gate at Salisbury, an ancient gate, is one of three which to this day are locked every night, enclosing Salisbury Cathedral and its surrounding ancient buildings from the rest of the city. Repair work to the cathedral spire has been said to involve 'a miracle of scaffolding', a special service being held when all was completed in readiness for the great operation. Bournemouth residents and visitors, over many years, make the pilgramage to one of our greatest cathedrals.

98. This is a beautiful postcard study by Judges, of the Lower Gardens, Bournemouth, issued in the late 1930s. The Lower Gardens have their southern entrance close to the Pavilion near the Pier approach, a long stretch of flower beds and shady paths. The whole is enhanced by the Bourne Stream running through. Thousands of holidaymakers over the years remember the pleasant days spent alongside this 3½ mile long rivulet. Some have walked its length from Alder Road, Parkstone, to the point where it disappears under the Pier approach and into the sea.

99. Waverley, known as 'the world's last sea-going paddle steamer', has made calls at Bournemouth and in the last summer we were there, 1989, sailed from Bournemouth, Swanage, Weymouth, Southampton, Southsea and Worthing between 3rd and 19th September. Her magnificent steam engines in operation with skilled engineers at the controls have fascinated generations. This superb survivor of the great age of steam is operated by the Paddle Steamer Preservation Society, Waverley's sister steamer being Kingswear Castle.

100. S.S. Queen, seen on this 1910 postcard, was Dutch built and bought by the Cosens Company from Weymouth. A jetty was constructed at Bournemouth, hoping to attract such paddle steamers as Queen, but it was of poor construction and soon swept away. During the war the Cosens fleet were fortunate, suffering no losses, but other companies were less so. The Gracie Fields, for example, launched by the singer and comedienne herself in 1936, was lost at Dunkirk. By the 1940s paddle steamers were on the decline and we must be thankful for such as Waverley.

101. The town and church of Churchtown date back to Saxon times. The rivers Avon and Stow meet at this point where the ancient foundation grew up, to flow into Christchurch Bay. In the recording of the town in Domesday Book it was entered as Twynham, from its position between two waters. When William the Conqueror crushed the Saxons and proclaimed himself King there were only 21 houses on which a yearly tax of sixpence was paid. The High Street in 1900, with Hayward's Fancy Goods shop on the right, had changed little until the 20th century and Christchurch still has some reminders of antiquity in Ye Olde Eight Bells Shoppe A.D. 1450, and Ye Olde George Inn Coach House, an old coaching inn. Traditional Country Fairs are held in the New Forest at Ringwood with Adams Axe Men, the Beagles, falconry and the slippery pole recalling medieaval England.

102. Boscombe front from the pier features in a good picture postcard from 1930. Before development, on the southern or seaward side of the road a great pine wood used to stand, part of which had to go to make way for residences. Hotels and boarding houses sprang up as time went on, shops were necessary as hawkers, beach traders etc. who from the first had been a nuisance, were forbidden on the beaches. From 1900 there was strict control over all beach trading and standards laid down for bathing attire. The ladies had to wear a costume, tunic or blouse, reaching from neck to knees, with belt and knickerbocker drawers. They also had to use a tent or bathing machine at all times except at two places, Boscombe Chine and Durley Chine, but only then between 7 a.m. and 1 p.m.

103. A very good postcard, showing the approach to the pier from another standpoint, dates from the 1940s or late 1930s. Under a magnifying glass, the price of ices at the kiosk in the foreground is hard to believe. A crowded day, possibly at midsummer, and no queue for the penny cornets! During the Second World War the pier was considered by some to be a danger as enemy troops could have landed there. A local army commander blew up the entrance to render it useless as an approach from the sea. After the war the pier was rebuilt for the people's enjoyment once more and by the 1980s a new pier entrance with restaurants and amusement arcades had been incorporated.

Boscombe Pier

104. Another pier, this one Boscombe in 1905 which was built by private enterprise in 1886, symbol of rivalry as local men, keen on Boscombe's progress, considered it indispensable if Boscombe was to compete with Bournemouth, near neighbours that they were. Archibald Smith, a Boscombe man, designed it and the Boscombe Pier Company persuaded Lady Shelley to drive the first pile of a splendid iron construction built by the Waterloo Foundry of Poole. The Duke of Argyll opened it in 1889. Unfortunately it was never a success. A 65 foot whale, cast up on the beach, was exhibited on the pier decking but excited little interest and in 1940 the zealous Army Commander had Boscombe Pier 'blown up' as he had Bournemouth Pier for the war's duration. However, it rose again in the 1950s, with a roller-skating rink.

105. A splendid view of the pier from East Cliff in the 1930s shows also the steep cliff face and carriageway below. That Bournemouth can still offer two piers for the enjoyment of visitors is something to be proud of as pier upkeep is now expensive. We must not forget that the town at one time had three piers. Southbourne Pier, built in 1888, did not last long as, unlike the other two, it had no protection from the Purbeck Hills. Originally costing £4,000, it was destroyed by gales in 1901. Attempts to develop a resort at Southbourne failed in 1883 when a Land Company built 300 feet of esplanade and six stately homes beneath the cliffs. Crashing seas and westerly winds caused two French vessels to founder, but the 'lost' resort still has reference in the porter's remembered ring: 'Christchurch for Southbourne-on-Sea'.

106. Piers put one in mind of concert parties, indispensable for seaside resorts. Although Bournemouth strove for the genteel, quieter image, the Queen magazine reported in 1910 on the prevalence along the south coast of '... nigger, musical performers of varying degrees of discord, overcrowded wagonettes and steam trips, pier entertainments and the rest which affect adversely those with finer nerves. Young ladies give themselves up to abandon on the piers'. It is not certain that this group of performers appeared at Bournemouth but, this card having been found locally, it is possible that the Fez Olympians did shows on Bournemouth Pier in 1894. Other concert parties were Birchmore and Linden's Pierrots and the Gay Cadets. Punch and Judy always 'pulled in the crowds'.

107. The West Cliff in 1919 still has much of the original terrain. The shelter offered by trees and bushes, besides the natural advantage of the lee of the Purbecks, was what 'Made Winter into Summer', or 'where the season never ends', slogans that promoted the town, backed by medical men who came after Dr. Granville. Another area of heathland at Wallisdown was used for the Talbot Model Village, to benefit people less well off. Miss Charlotte Talbot in the 1830s was concerned with their welfare and arranged for cottages of red or yellow brick, each surrounded by a garden where vegetables and fruit could be grown to help a small income. Later on, farms, a school and almshouses, designed by Mr. Creeke, were added to the small complex.

108. Written from the Beacon Hotel, West Cliff, in 1918 this lovely postcard's message reads: 'We have had a very pleasant holiday here and we all like Bournemouth.' The beach, looking west, shows the popularity of paddling, bathing and boating. The Bournemouth beach for these visitors extended to Hengistbury on the east and to Sandbanks near Poole Harbour, six miles of clean, firm sand, bounded by cliffs. Even at high tide there was plenty of room between the sea and cliffs and if exceptionally rough seas blew up, the parades were safe and the cliffs so sloping, it was quite unlikely that any visitor could be cut off by the tide. The cliffs shown in the photograph are about 100 feet high.

The Zig-Zag Footpath Bournemouth.

109. The zig-zag footpath at Bournemouth is still a well-known feature, affording long and gentle cliff descent. This postcard written from 'the hut on the sands' is glowing in praise of Bournemouth. In July 1909, the date of the card, visitors could read newspapers fixed onto the walls of Mr. Wells's fried fish shop as they waited. Gray's, Bakers, at Parkstone, sold penny bread puddings and ginger cakes for a farthing. Shops remained open until 11 p.m. and at 9 p.m. some fruiterers would sell remaining fruit very cheaply as it was liable to go bad. Some visitors in small apartment houses brought in their own food for the landlady to prepare, thus obtaining as cheap a holiday as possible.

110. In 1884 the long cutting through Meyrick Park and Talbot Woods was excavated by contractors Mowlem for doubling the line between Branksome and Poole. Branksome railway viaduct, completed the same year, involved the tipping of tons of sand and gravel to form embankments. The chief engineer on this project learned his profession under the famous Isambard Kingdom Brunel. This postcard from 1930 shows Branksome Chine and the Solarium.

111. Over the years the names of some lesser roads have changed. Gas Works Road became Bourne Valley Road, in the neighbourhood of Bourne Moor Farm and Alder Farm. The original cottages built amidst heath and heather would be thatched. At Parkstone early dwellings known as soddys were built of turves and clay. An old farm photograph that has survived from the area (though the farm and farmhand are not known) is this 1902 postcard of two horses fitted with what resemble primitive or home-made blinkers, tied on. The horses were less likely to be startled if they looked ahead with no left to right digressions in their sights.

112. Scalpin's Court at Poole during demolition of old tenements in 1925 led to the discovery that the site was once where the Hall of the Fraternity of St. George, an old lay-guild of Poole, had been. A 1535 fireplace was revealed and when tenement partitions were removed, the Guildhall itself, 40 feet long. This postcard showing the Old Town House has altered Scalpin to Scaplen, showing how names alter over the years, possibly by word of mouth. In this interesting town are the old pump, three lots of almshouses, some dating back to Henry V, and a Quaker Meeting House in Langland Street, built in 1690.

113. The Harbour Office on Poole Quay was built with pillars, sundials and a memorial tablet to a mayor who lived in the 18th century. Beneath is the Woolhouse, originally a 13th century chapel, which in the 15th century was used by renegades and pirates. The Lord Nelson Inn is supposedly where Nelson called to use one of the rooms on official business. This postcard from 1929 shows some of the masted barques and brigantines, once a common sight. On the east quay at the time of this photograph were the works of Messrs. Carter, Stabler and Adams, forerunners of Poole Pottery. Poole then sent valuable clay in large quantities to the Potteries in Staffordshire.

114. Swans in Poole Park occupy two lakes, one of fresh water, one salt, the latter as a result of a railway embankment cutting off a part of the harbour. It is a well-wooded area with model yachting, cricket, bowling and tennis. Thomas Hardy used Poole as 'Havenport' in his Wessex Tales. Philip Henry Gosse, one resident, became a famous naturalist, an authority on marine invertebrates. A master mariner, Peter Joliffe, captured a French privateer in 1694 for which he was presented with a gold medal on a chain, by King William III.

115. Except on Sundays, a regular steamboat service ran between Bournemouth and Swanage in the 1920s. 'Of all the steamboat excursions the most frequent and best patronised are those to Swanage,' printed the Ward Lock Guide of 1920. The postcard, from before that date, shows the Clock Tower and a fine paddle steamer that may be from Bournemouth. The Tilly Whim Caves attracted visitors, although they were warned of dangers and entered this haunt of smugglers at their own risk. Another attraction was the Great Globe made of Portland stone, 10 feet in diameter and 40 tons in weight. Inscribed on huge stone walls is information about the world.

Bournemouth Gardens.   JWS 174

116. This 1904 postcard of Central Gardens must, I feel, be included as it shows a patient donkey pulling a bath chair guided by an attendant. A fine day, so the hood is not up and the occupant can enjoy the sight of colourful, orderly flower beds and the fountain which continues to feature in photographs fifty years later. At the time of this postcard there was great demand in Bournemouth for domestic servants in the houses of wealthy people. The Wharncliffe High Class Registry Office, Boscombe, proprietress Miss Armstrong, was applied to 'for all classes of Domestic Servant, Nurses, Governesses, Companions and Helps'. It is also interesting to see that as early as 1901 there was a Mail Order House, Spratt and Company of Old Christchurch Road, Bournemouth.

117. Before the construction of Undercliffe Drive shown here in 1908 it was customary to allow communal entertainments to be held on the sands on Bank Holidays. Many changes have taken place. The site of the Rustic Bridge, 1863, became the Bournemouth Arcade. Number 1, Westover Villas became the site of Messrs. Austin Reed. Cliff Cottage, one of the earliest houses to be built, then occupied 3½ acres of wooded land. Stone was quarried at Charborough, the same as nearby Almer Church. One owner of Cliff Cottage was William Fryer, a Wimborne banker. John S. Warley Sawbridge was another early owner who in 1827 married Jane Frances Grosvenor. Cliff Cottage was sometimes let to visitors, the most distinguished visitor being Charles Darwin in 1862. It was pulled down in 1876.

The Cliffs and Sea, Bournemouth

118. Madame Florence, antique dealer of 103, Old Christchurch Road and 43, Commercial Road, was able in 1914 to boast 'patronised by royalty'. Boscombe is still an area of antique shops. Very early memories of residents who have lived in Bournemouth all their lives and had stories passed down to them from parents, aunts, uncles and grandparents, recall that goats used to be kept on the heathland. It is said that Eric Rose who later became a Mayor of Bournemouth bought a goat for one shilling from Frank Purdy. People in outlying areas were allowed to keep pigs. Mr. Watts, blacksmith, sold his iron hoops for a halfpenny for children to bowl along the street. In Gladstone Road was Bugler's Bakery, famous for spicy, sticky, Hot Cross Buns at Easter. These were all memories when this postcard was printed in 1930, one of many real photographs transmitted to postcards.

119. Even before the turn of the century it was urged in letters to the Bournemouth Graphic that the Council should consider urgently the making of Undercliff Drive. It was 'about all that was necessary to place Bournemouth in the forefront of English health resorts and would enable us to compete with the attractions of the Riviera'. Negotiations with Sir George Meyrick resulted in 1903 in a lease by which rights and interests in the Bournemouth cliffs and foreshore were vested in Bournemouth Corporation for 999 years. The first section was completed in 1911. Further sections were finished over the next two years, including the Undercliff Drive to Boscombe, opened by the Earl and Countess of Malmesbury. That it was in use before the official date of opening is shown in this card franked 12th July 1909, written by Betty, who was urgently requesting that her 'visiting cards' be forwarded.

120. 'We're losing fast the good old days of rattling wheels and gallant greys. The English stage and high-bred teams will soon exist but in our dreams.' So wrote Eliza Cook about the passing of the stagecoach. Horses were actually colour-matched on the important main-road routes to Bath, Malvern Wells or Gloucester. The coaches had splendid names: The Magnet Safety Coach; Mercury; Vivid; Royal Veteran; Royal Pilot; Aurora. The Royal Albiontic Hotel in Brighton regularly received Mr. Chandos Pole's coach and four. In Bournemouth's early days was the Tally Ho, but the fastest coaches were the Shrewsbury Wonder and the Manchester Telegraph. As early as 1840 daily horse-drawn coaches called at Bournemouth on their way between Southampton, Poole, Dorchester and Weymouth. Henry Laidlaw who operated Tally Ho lived in a house which later became the Dalkeith Hotel in Old Christchurch Road. The old photograph shows the most famous coachman of all operating to the south coast in the 18th century, James Selby, who died only a few months after winning a wager for his master on a run to Brighton that made history.

121. Genteel Bournemouth in its coming of age may well have played down the presence of the king of smugglers. Isaac Gulliver in the 18th century who unloaded goods from his fleet of 15 luggers and, using pack horses, made across heathland to Kinson where the contraband was stored. He considered himself a gentleman smuggler who had never killed anyone though he was known all down the coast as far as Cornwall. He bought a farm at Lilliput in Poole. Dean Swift, who lived in Lilliput for a time, wrote 'Gulliver's Travels' there. The house that Isaac used at Kinson was pulled down in 1930 to reveal a large, secret room 10 feet above the chimney piece. A trap door entrance led to a vast cellar and a network of tunnels. At Bournemouth, Boscombe and Branksome, Gulliver and his men, attired in farmers' smocks, unloaded brandy, tea, silk, tobacco and lace. If any customs men were quickly espied appearing on the flat heathland, goods could be hustled down the deep wells which were to be found all over the heath.

122. Lady Emily Toler was one of Bournemouth's titled visitors from the days of Queen Victoria. In thatched cottages were staying the Duke and Duchess of Montrose, the Duke of Argyll, Queen Marie-Amelia of France and the novelist Bulwer Lytton. Queen Victoria was known to recommend Bournemouth to her favourite statesmen should they be in poor health. The first residential suburb was Springbourne, which was filled with smaller properties built for hotel staff, domestic servants, bricklayers and other members of the building trade, coachmen and stablehands. The gentry could not manage without these hewers of wood and drawers of water and they needed cheap housing to be able to work in Bournemouth.

123. The Tregonwell Arms some time about 1880 advertised 'good beds' and 'hot joints from 12.0 to 2.0'. It has many interesting hoardings which under the magnifying glass show up as: 'Photography notice – photographic studio'; 'Town Hall Concerts' and a list of locals' 'Stock in Trade'. An early travel guide of the 1840s printed: 'Bourne Cliff or Tregonwell's Bourne, about six miles from Christchurch, on the road to Poole, is a modern-built watering place. The sands are extensive and several bathing-machines are kept.' A photograph of the Tregonwell Arms, the erstwhile Tapps Arms, where it all started, is a good place to finish.